UNDERSTANDING

by Sandra Ziegler
illustrated by Jenny Williams

THE CHILD'S WORLD

Mankato, MN 56001

I like little Pussy,
  Her coat is so warm;
And if I don't hurt her,
  She'll do me no harm.

So I'll not pull her tail,
  Nor drive her away,
But Pussy and I
  Very gently will play.

—from "Little Pussy"
by Jane Taylor

Library of Congress Cataloging in Publication Data

Ziegler, Sandra, 1938-
    Understanding / by Sandra Ziegler ; illustrated by Jenny Williams.
      p. cm. — (What is it?)
    ISBN 0-89565-452-0
    1. Empathy—Juvenile literature. 2. Children—Conduct of Life.
I. Williams, Jenny, 1939-   II. Title.   III. Series.
BF575.E55Z54   1989
179'.9—dc19   88-23745
                                                      CIP

What is understanding?
Understanding is holding your cat
in a way that will not hurt her.

When your friend loses her purse,
and you help her look till she finds
it, that's understanding.

And so is sharing her joy when she
does.

"A little understanding" is what Mom
asks you to have when you want your
sister to play with you, but she has
to do her homework.

When your sister spills her milk . . .

understanding is not making fun of
her.

When you are coloring eggs and your sister drips blue coloring on your best yellow egg, understanding is saying, ''That's okay. Let's make it a polka-dot egg.''

When a friend slips and falls into a
mud puddle, understanding is helping
him up.

When you smile at a new girl in class, you are saying, "I know how you feel." That's understanding.

Choosing Juan to be on your "Hang-man" team, even if he is just learning English . . . that's understanding.

And so is hugging your friend when
her parakeet dies and she cries.

When your sister strikes out and
drops a fly ball, understanding is
saying, "You'll do better next time."

Understanding is letting your little sister sleep with you because she thinks a monster is under her bed.

When your sister is going to miss a
T.V. special because she promised to
rake leaves, understanding is saying,
"I know how you feel. I'll help you
so you will finish in time."

When a friend can't come to your birthday party because he has the chicken pox, understanding is sending over a piece of cake and a party hat.

If your friend isn't allowed to eat
sweets, understanding is saying,
"Let's both eat popcorn."

When Tracy's parents have told her
not to cross the street on her bike . . .

understanding is not crossing it on
yours.

Understanding is knowing how some-
one else feels . . .

and then treating him as you would
like to be treated.

Understanding is a special gift that people can give to each other.